"Tinhorn Gamblers and Prostitutes":

Vice in 19th century Council Bluffs

Ryan Roenfeld

A program presented to the Pottwattamie County

Genealogical Society in August 2014.

Council Bluffs finally got legal gambling towards the end of the 20th century with Las Vegas companies, bright lights, and buffets. Not so long ago, a city councilman got caught in a craigslist massage, Farrah Abraham got famous, and the city was named one of America's sexiest suburbs and 69th most dangerous city. So maybe nothing much has changed since Lady Luck rolled into Mormon Kanesville during the Gold Rush of '49 to set off a bawdy era when the city ran wide open with sins of all sorts that proved a playground for some of America's most notorious confidence men.

The response by pious Kanesville was predictable and in February 1852 the Mormon newspaper lamented that

"When the Church Council was our only tribunal here, we had no grog shops - Indians were not allowed to stalk abroad on this side, and vice and confusion were comparatively unknown..." Vice and confusion would become well known and provided a plump set-up for that select sort who prey on those with easy cash who were headed somewhere else. The newspapers called them "monte men" and "three-carders" and they found a comfortable roost right through the 1870s. Three-card monte is still played today but finding that one card out of the three is still a scam. There was also faro, the preferred game of the Old West now mostly forgotten. Faro isn't all that difficult to learn and you can win or lose everything on the draw of a single card. Odds against the house are pretty good too which is why you can't 'buck the tiger' in any casino today. The game was also easy to rig, especially with the right kind of dealer and special-ordered card-boxes.

The Mormons were all but gone by 1853 when the city officially became Council Bluffs and relied on $280 in revenue, most of it from licensing saloons since they couldn't tax squatter land titles. Amelia Bloomer's husband Dexter later wrote that then "every available building was ere long converted to a gambling or drinking hall" and William Gilbert called Council Bluffs "the poorest meanest dirty hole I ever saw…" on his way through. It was a hard town with the Ocean Wave, the Gem, the Bluff Saloon, the Buna Vista, and the Emporium Exchange, which had its own Bowling Saloon, all right on Broadway. In February 1854 the Council Bluffs Chronotype newspaper reported that there were a dozen murderers at the city jail, including two teenagers who killed a policeman and a 15 year old boy who shot a man "for no particular reason." One Council Bluffs scam in 1854 was called Omaha City that the ferry company ran out of the Pacific House hotel. That was the same year Council Bluffs residents got legal title to their squatter claims with the 80 acre "Old Town Plat" a maze compared the modern street grid.

Prostitution always had a place as well through a well established system of kick-backs. While technically illegal, the madams, pimps, and prostitutes just paid a monthly fine, a ready supply of municipal revenue and easy fodder for politicians and newspapers to muck up during elections and slow news days. In June 1858, the Council Bluffs *Bugle* newspaper noted "Another disgraceful row" at the "Flat Roof: a house of ill fame" during which one man was shot "in a delicate, but not dangerous part of the body". Two others received knife wounds.

The Civil War brought the Union Pacific and Ben Marks whose simple discovery when the Hell-on-Wheels hit Cheyenne was the start of the big-store confidence swindle later refined in Council Bluffs. The city grew from 2,000 residents in 1860 to almost 8,000 by 1867, the year the Chicago & Northwestern railroad was completed from Chicago west to the Missouri River with a depot at West Broadway and 11th Street. Between the depot and downtown was Lower Broadway: six blocks of cafes, saloons, hotels, groceries, brothels, and gambling dens.

How could all this carrying on without the city's approval? It couldn't but one should remember that through the 19th century most elected officials weren't born here, they came from somewhere else. It seemed impossible to bust up such an entrenched system, especially if it would raise taxes. City aldermen were still elected by wards and made most of the real decisions of municipal government as the mayor was a power, figurehead, and scapegoat all at once and Council Bluffs would have two dozen mayors in the 44 years between 1867 and 1911.

Sporadic sweeps continued by those determined to clean up Council Bluffs for good. One raid took place in April 1867 when the *Nonpareil* reported the arrest of "inmates of several houses of ill-construction". Josephine Smith, Nettie Cook, Emily Longfellow (the newspaper called her "as short as a gimlet handle"), Angie Smith, Annie Wright, Annie Furier, Nellie Shepherd, Maggie Woods, and Jennie Baker were all fined $20 each and those who could not come up with the fine were "donated the use of the 'cellar parlor' of the jail, for a few days or longer...Such is life." The next month the *Nonpareil* moralized about the "growing evil in this city" of "drunken men and women on our streets. There is no use disguising the fact that almost every day in the past week, men beastly drunk were seen staggering along the Broadway pavements, and on Saturday some women gave us a like infernal exhibition of their depravity, not only by appearing drunk but by fighting on Madison Street. It is no credit to a city to have these things published, but our duty as journalist, who has the welfare of the city at heart will not allow us to longer remain silent over such shocking enormities."

By 1869 Council Bluffs had around 8,500 residents and 39 saloons, roughly one bar for every 217 or so residents. There was the Court House at Main and Pearl, the Eureka, the City Brewery Garden, and the Tivoli Gardens on the east side of Franklin between Voorhis and Platner Streets. The Dew Drop, Western Star Hall, Short's Saloon, "To Old Fred", and the Chicago and Douglas House hotel saloons were all on Lower Broadway.

Other forms of entertainment were readily available and on May Day 1869 the *Nonpareil* announced that the police "have made the Cyprians and their alderman abettors flutter again" as "Matters had begun to get rather more lively than healthy." The newspaper went on to describe how "warrant after warrant issued for the apprehension of the 'fair women' and 'brave men' who ply their hellish avocations on the West End." Those hauled before the judge included "French Moll", Polly, Ida Tucker, Harry Williams,

Sallie Freeman, Jane Spencer, Jim Coats, Frank Master, Lorin Kennedy who "marched up and paid" for his "affectionate wife" Mollie, Mollie Scott, Kate Hatfield, Liz Hicks, Amelia Johnson, and May Dale and "Indian Moll", both from the brothel dubbed the "Iron Clad".

"Cyprians" seems a quaint synonym for prostitute but in spite of the crackdown the next month the *Nonpareil* claimed that "men of sober habits and respectable deportment have been inquiring whether or not Cyprians owned and controlled this city". Once their fines were paid the women returned "to their infamous work with good cheer and a willingness that the devil himself would shudder at to assume in a desperate case." The newspaper once again listed those hauled before the City Recorder to pay their fines: William Strope and Mollie Strope "dubbed for short, in this community, as 'French Moll'", John Rhodes, Harry Williams, "Indian Moll", Harry Wilson "and woman", Flora and Lizzie Hicks, "Kate", Em Brown, Amelia Johnson, "Sophia", Mat Henry, Lillie Toker, May Dale, Lara Bradley, Jim Coats, Frank Master, Addie Hughes, Daniel Haynes, and two fellows who gave their names as "James Jones and John Smith". The newspaper clucked that it was "sorry that the Jones's and Smith's families, not common in this world, should have in each of them a black sheep." William H. Strope was listed in the J. M. Wolfe city directory for 1869-70 as residing on the northwest corner of West Broadway and 14th Street and his given occupation in the 1870 census was "whoremaster". His frequent companion "French Moll" was listed in the 1871 city directory as "Ms. M. Strope" on the south side of what is now 1st Avenue near 14th Street.

The 1870 census was the first to report that 16 year old Omaha had grown bigger than Council Bluffs while the "circumstances of another fallen woman, and her abandonment of all hope of reclamation and of virtue, for a life of infamy and degradation" appeared in the *Nonpareil* that January. The "young woman - girl, in fact, for she is not yet eighteen - has been a servant in a number of families in this city." An orphan, her "first step after taking her fearful resolution was to enter a low concern not a great ways from Upper Broadway, on the south side." Her employers found her there and used threats "to return from this low hell and return to her place." However, she "concluded to take another leap and packing up her clothes...avowing that a dance house in the lower part of the city would be her future home." The "low concern" alluded to by the newspaper was apparently the "Rotten Row" that grew on West Pierce Street between 1st Street and Park Avenue. Yes, the worst of the city's red-light district was right between Broadway Methodist and St. Peter's Catholic church.

On April 18, 1870 an item in the *Bugle* newspaper noted that "As we were coming up Broadway Saturday...we saw the door of a saloon opened and a man shoved out on the sidewalk, seemingly in a helpless condition from the effects of the 'benzine,' or other poisonous mixtures he had obtained in the mill through which he had been run and 'bolted' out the door, They had got his 'last dime' and had no further use for him."

There were 35 saloons listed in Beech and Gwyer's

1871 directory along with five billiard halls, a bowling alley, and 24 hotels. That was the year Susan B. Anthony spoke in town and profits off prostitution sparked a feud between the city's two rival newspapers. The *Nonpareil*'s accusations that the *Council Bluffs Times* "slops over in fulsome praise of the city authorities for keeping up the revenues of the city by regular levies upon the houses of ill-fame, and their inmates." The newspaper disparaged its competition's claim that "the trade of these unfortunates is just as much a necessity in any ordinary community as any other trade" and instead declared that the regular fines paid by prostitutes "proves that the city authorities are engaged in the disreputable practice of levying blackmail upon a lot of 'unfortunates' engaged in a business that is a necessary adjunct of our prosperity as a city! Is there the least mite of justice in singling out an 'unfortunate' class for such exactions, and making them pledge that their first sinful wages shall be given up to pay the city for the privilege of carrying on their business?" The *Nonpareil* called it a "burning shame for the city of Council Bluffs to bring these 'workers for our good' before the bar of justice; impose a fine upon them that they are unable to pay; and then dismiss them to houses of prostitution, with strict injunctions to pay the city the amount of their assessment from the first money they earn in their disreputable calling!"

The newspaper also dismissed the claims that "when information is filed against a house of ill-fame, the authorities do their duty, and pull it" and noted that these "houses are not regularly complained of once a month - and all at the same time!" Instead, the newspaper reported that "conclusively that this work of 'pulling' these houses is wholly the proceeding of the city authorities, for the purpose of raising money...The City Government should be sustained in some other manner." As it was, "If it is decided that we must tolerate prostitution as a necessary evil, then let us cease to 'compound' with these unfortunates; and refrain from levying blackmail upon them. If they are here for our good, let us not make them prostitute themselves to fill the coffers of the city treasury. If their 'trade is as necessary to this community as any other trade,' let is be placed upon the same free footing."

Two days later on February 18th the *Nonpareil* gave the details of Chief of Police Bump's report of the 29 arrests during the past month with $33.85 the "amount of cash collected" and an outstanding $86.15 "assessed and uncollected". That included one arrest for drunkenness and

16 for "inmates of houses of ill-fame".

A sarcastic letter printed by the *Nonpareil* concerned a recent *Times* article that reported only one of "the unfortunates living in the lower part of town" was able to pay her fine. The "others the city had kindly given credit until they could earn the money" and were allowed to go work off their fines. The letter in the *Nonpareil* noted that "times are hard and money scarce, and the 'unfortunates' might be driven away, and the City Treasury be short of the usual five or ten dollars a head assessments." Instead, "would it not be a good plan for the city to send off to Chicago or New York and bring on a large number, and establish more houses, and thereby receive a larger income- for the more unfortunates the city has, the more money the authorities will receive." This plan would "cost but little, and when once here they will be no expense to the city" and they would pay for their own boarding, clothes, and "pay their stated profit or income tax every month regularly; and the trouble of collecting costs nothing. All the police have to do is to get their names and the number employed, and give them to the Recorder, and he makes out the receipts, and the police collect the money at the house!" This would be a "big thing for the city" and "if it is profitable and pays well on a small scale, it must on a larger one, in proportion. And, as what can we do to pay the expenses of the city best, and save expense to the city, is soon to come before the people as an issue of importance...."

The newspaper continued that "Time and again have the police visited these houses and collected the 'levy'-not because the public had suffered from the 'unruly or outrageous' conduct of the cyprians...but simply to put money into the city Treasury." The newspaper did "not despair of finally stopping these illegal levies, and shall continue to blaze away at the practice until it is abandoned." The practice would continue openly for most of the next 40 years and likely longer than that.

The Union Pacific bridge to Omaha opened in March 1872 when the *Nonpareil* reported "the gamblers have become so polite on the trains in this vicinity that they frequently reproach travelers by calling them cowards, family men, greenhorns, etc., when they refuse to play three-card monte." The bunch of monte men who worked the trains in and out of Council Bluffs and Omaha was loosely dubbed the Canada Bill Jones gang. Canada Bill was supposed to have been born in a gypsy tent in England but became a regular on the Mississippi River steamboats and mastered the persona of the total rube.

Gambler George Devol described him as a "medium-sized, chicken-headed, tow-haired sort of a man with mild blue eyes, and a mouth nearly from ear to ear, who walked with a shuffling, half-apologetic sort of a gait, and who, when his countenance was in repose, resembled an idiot". Canada Bill had a "squeaking, boyish voice, and awkward, gawky manners, and a way of asking fool questions and putting on a good natured sort of a grin, that led everybody to believe that he was the rankest kind of a sucker - the greenest sort of a country jake. Woe to the man who picked him up, though." Likewise, the 1883 *History of Pottawattamie County* dubbed the "notorious Canada Bill, the most expert gambler in the West" as a "tall, ungainly, sallow, stoop shouldered individual" who wore "a slouch hat drawn over his face" and "spoke with the twang of a Texas cattle drover...assuming this role when acting as a capper for his gang, never failed to secure his victim." Some of the more notable quotes now attributed to Canada Bill include: "It's immoral to let a sucker keep his money", "Suckers have no business with money anyhow", "A Smith and Wesson beats four aces", and when confronted by an obviously rigged faro game he replied "I know it's crooked, but it's the only game in town." In its salad days Canada Bill's empire supposedly included a variety of shady hotels and saloons in Omaha where suckers would be directed for fleecing from the trains pulling in and out of Council Bluffs and Omaha.

In September 1872 the *Nonpareil* reported that Canada Bill became "acquainted with a sympathetic minister to the amount of $500" on a Union Pacific train. He "was assisted by his little 'keerds.'" That issue also related that the "three card monte men took in one hundred dollars on one of the trains coming into this city, yesterday evening" but "as soon as their operations were discovered, a brakeman stopped the little game." The 1907 *History of Pottawattamie County* recalled the "bunco men" of this era as "men of good address and had numbers of friends" who "gave liberally to any benevolent scheme" that would benefit the town. One later profile of Canada Bill noted that he had "thirty or forty men as decoys or 'cappers'" but "Only once in his life, so far as it is known, did he suffer a worsting, and that was at the hands of an Iowa farmer, who deluded him into paying for a wagon load of cheese one day in Council Bluffs. The aroma of that cheese still clings to him, and is the one sore spot in his memory no one can touch without ruffling his temper."

There were 29 saloons listed in the 1873 Corbett, Hoye and Company directory. The Tivoli Gardens had moved to Broadway and Ben Marks was living at the Bryant House hotel. Canada Bill was buried in a pauper's grave in Pennsylvania in 1880 but nothing much changed at Council Bluffs. In June 1880 the *Nonpareil* noted a "General Round-Up" and the arrest of a half dozen "women of the town" along with a few gamblers. Chief of Police Jackson claimed "that a great deal of complaint has been made against the houses of ill-fame" while the gamblers had "not been conducting business exactly within the rules and regulations of the police." Those charged with "conducting and keeping a house of ill-fame" were "Josie Wood, Stella Long, Lou Scott, E. Hubbert and wife, Ann Butterfield, Grace Belford, Bell Clover, Anna Morris and Anna Berry".

Belle Clover had a long career in Council Bluffs and her cathouse was located on the southwest corner of West Broadway and 8th Street, now a turning lane. She was once described by the Omaha newspaper as a "sweet daughter of Hades" and one time took her entire house of girls out to Cheyenne to work a spell. She came back to Council Bluffs though and had a long-term abusive relationship with George Gerspacher, manager of the notorious Union Avenue hotel west down the street.

Perhaps the town's most reputable house of ill repute was Stella Long's, situated at 247 and then at 151 West Broadway. Her house at 151 was right across the street from the historic 100 block. In the early 1880s Lou Scott's brothel was a block southeast along West Pierce's "Rotten

Row" in what one Omaha newspaper called it the "burnt district" of Council Bluffs. There was also Josie Woods at Market and Vine Streets, now adjacent or underneath the old Midlands Mall.

In June 1883 the *Omaha Daily Bee* newspaper reported the return of Doc Baggs to the area "accompanied by eight companion spirits". Doc Baggs was "a well known character in the days of Canada Bill, and has made a record scarcely less notorious out west". Doc Baggs formerly lived in Council Bluffs on the east side of 8th Street between West Broadway and Mynster Street and was the master of the "gold brick" scam.

That December the *Bee* reported that during a two day buffet a businessman "squandered $300 in a 'high time' in a house of prostitution" in Council Bluffs. Chief of Police Field reported 60 arrests that month and the Omaha newspaper wrote "one would think from the report that there were no gamblers in the city, but few prostitutes, and scarcely any vagrants, but all citizens know that gambling places are running more open than the police station, while prostitutes and vagrants are numerous...In no city, even in the wild west, are gambling houses and houses of ill fame run so openly" as in Council Bluffs. The Omaha newspaper claimed "Council Bluffs is letting the gambling houses, prostitutes, variety shows, etc, go as they please" and considered it "nearly time for another city house cleaning and spasm of reform".

In 1885 the *Bee* reported that the "keepers of the house of prostitution" paid their $29 monthly fine after the marshal "served notices on the girls" and "expected them to come up with about $10 each, and unless they respond promptly they are to be arrested and locked up." Another *Bee* article concerned "a man named Charles Everett" who worked for the Milwaukee railroad and lived in Coon Rapids. Everett came to Council Bluffs "to hunt up his wayward wife, who had entered upon a life of shame here." The woman refused to leave with him but then in "repent, and has written him to send her money, and she shall reform." Everett was not the first or last to came to Council Bluffs for that same reason. Chief Skinner had also "ordered the saloons to keep closed yesterday" which was an a decree that "came so unexpectedly that many did not have time to get locks and bolts for the back doors".

      This attempt to close the saloons on Sunday was "not

very generally observed, the front doors being pretty well shut up, but the rear doors being slightly ajar." Eight saloons were reportedly open on Sunday but the Omaha newspaper thought the mayor would merely point to a lack of direction from the aldermen while "claiming all the glory among the temperance folks for taking this stand against the saloons."

That November there was another "Attempt to Rid the City of Hard Cases" reported by the *Bee* with a "rounding up" of "vags, tinhorn gamblers and dirty prostitutes" in Council Bluffs. This seemed to be "not resulting in much." Most wouldn't be tried, others would leave town but return soon enough, and "few have been fined, and fewer yet have been compelled to pay their fine." The *Bee* newspaper described the "disappointment of the police" who had gone "to the trouble of making a raid" on Pierce Street. There was a woman named Hattie Anderson "who had a husband in Omaha" and put her kids in "a charitable institution" to "become a denizen of 'Rotten Row'." The raid on Mrs. Anderson's also found "a young girl" and "the notorious 'Sandy' Knight, who used to be an Omaha policeman". In the hubbub the police could not swear who was where in the house and all of them were let go. Also raided "was the house kept by the colored family over which Minnie Johnson lives" which found "Johnson and his wife, a colored girl hid under the bed, a white woman, and three white men." It was "the difficulty of getting just the proof required caused a general release on technical grounds." The *Bee* noted that "It seems impossible for these disreputable places to be cleaned out. That part of Pierce Street known as 'Rotten Row' is rightly named. It is a disgrace to the city. It should be cleaned up, but there is little encouragement from the police to make arrests if those who make this section so disreputable are to be turned loose."

On November 17 the *Bee* reported that the police had "'rounded up' several good sized herds" as the "disreputable part of Pierce Street known as 'rotten row' was visited, and about a dozen women, black and white, were gathered in. Frank Adams' house was also pulled and a large number of colored gentlemen arrested" along with "a gathering in of several stray ones from off the streets". There were 40 cases in court, "most of them charged with vagrancy, which covers a variety of sins. Gambling, prostitution, etc., as well as being without visible means of support, constitute vagrancy." Several of the black men were let go if they had someone there to vouch for them. The eleven women in court had their "cases were disposed of in various ways" as "Some were continued, others were discharged, and a few were put on their trial." Of course, none "of them admitted being guilty, and nearly everyone claimed to be 'working out'." That prompted the judge to ask the marshal to "bring up the hired girls." Also, "May Alley was found guilty of being drunk, but her best man paid the fine." The question in the *Bee* remained "Why this sudden raiding?" which was "in accordance with the order of the mayor" and perhaps this "spurt of reform" was due to certain revelations in the "Chicago papers".

On January 2, 1886 the *Bee* noted the return to Council Bluffs of the "tall, slim figure that used to hang about the doors of the gambling houses" known by "de gang" as "Long Dave". It seemed that he'd spent most of the winter in the Omaha jail for being an "all round crook". January 1886 was a rough winter with horse-drawn sleds used for public transportation and the *Bee* reported on a prostitute from Belle Clover's who "claims to be unable to pay her monthly fine". She spent her days in jail but then "returns home to her meals and lodgings" and presumably to work off her debt to the city on her back. That month the newspaper also reported on 15 year old Ada Griffin who ran away from Eastport, Iowa to a Council Bluffs "house of prostitution". Eastport was across the river from Nebraska City and Ms. Griffin claimed that she was "driven from home by the abusiveness of her father, and refuses to return."

Another form of abuse was shown in August 1886 when Stella Long had Jennie Palmer arrested "for running away with mortgaged property". Ms. Palmer was found innocent but according to the *Bee*, she'd been charged with "two other lady boarders at Stella Long's" who gave "chattel mortgages on their clothing" and were released. This was a few days after "they escaped from the house during the night" and Ms. Palmer "went to Belle Clover's, taking her clothing with her." That caused Stella Long to send out a police officer "to gobble up all her clothing" and "even the dress which the girl had on her back was stripped from her." Although Ms. Long had all the clothes "nothing but imprisonment would satisfy the irate landlady."

Old Mother Turner was another Council Bluffs madam whose house was near Horne's Park and no history of those years could fail to mention Richard Baker, better known as "Texas". "Texas" was Council Bluffs' black pimp during the 1880s who had a shack near the Chicago & Northwestern passenger depot, an interest in "Rotten Row", and his own gang of "colored wrecks". "Texas" also had a habit of getting in trouble, much like the unnamed farm boy who found his way into the *Bee* newspaper in May 1886 after he was lured into a Council Bluffs gambling house for "stud horse poker" and then robbed. A few days later Chief of Police Matthews outlawed "hazard, keno, and stud poker" from Council Bluffs. At the same time the long-time gambling house on West Broadway over the Phoenix Saloon had moved downstairs to keep up with competition. After all, "all the other gambling is done on the first floor" around town and they would save $100 a month in rent.

      More nefariousness seemed afoot by early July 1886 when the Nonpareil reported that "screams were heard issuing from a room over a saloon on Lower Broadway" while "parties below hastened upstairs to a room occupied by 'Carrie,' a woman of the town." Although her door was locked the "screams of "Murder! help!' caused the affrighted parties to break to the door down". However, instead of "someone in the hands of an assassin" they discovered "a married woman of this city giving the prostitute a severe thrashing." "Carrie" had a "black eye, a bad scratch on one breast made with a crochet needle and other marks of violence on her body." Her assailant, after she "could recover her breath", told them that "she had caught the woman with her husband several times and warned her that blood would flow if it was repeated." The newspaper speculated that the affair would not "get to police headquarters" as "'Carrie' has folded her tent and gone over to Omaha."

Another instance when Stella Long was no woman to be trifled with was reported by the *Bee* in September 1886 after a "man yesterday reported that he had been robbed of his pocket-book containing $50 and some valuable papers". This was after he paid a visit to "the sporting house of Stella Long on Broadway above the Ogden House." The man "refused to swear out a warrant against the girl in whose company he had been, as he did not care to give publicity to the case and would rather lose the $50..." That was followed by the story "A Pocketbook Found" relating that a pocket-book "containing valuable papers" owned by "W. B. Pierce, of Shelby, Ia" had been "discovered on Pierce Street in the rear of Stella Long's" by "one of the 'fairest of the row' who handed the pocket-book with the papers to Deputy Marshal White." Stella Long was emphatic that no one was "robbed of $50 the other night by one of the 'faeries' in her house". Instead, the *Bee* now claimed that it was a man from Council Bluffs who had been robbed, not "a stranger in the city", and that he had been robbed by a man, not a woman, but the victim still refused to swear out a complaint.

That month the *Bee* also reported on "a girl who is an inmate of a house of prostitution on Broadway, going under the name of Etta Smith..." Ms. Smith had "concluded to go to her home in three weeks" and "has given good reasons for not wishing to return" as "her brother-in-law has returned to his home in Nebraska for the present." A few weeks later *Bee* reported on Ella Smith, "one of the young ladies at Stella Long's boarding house", who had "left last night for the west, to start anew, and to try and live a different life." She was from Marshalltown, Iowa and it was her brother who had "traced her here" to Council Bluffs. He returned and "prevailed upon her to start on the road to reform" and "will provide her a home". Ms. Smith "being heartily weary of a life of shame, promises to redeem herself."

Maybe Ms Smith did and maybe she didn't but so it would go through the first decade of the 20th century when the house of cards finally came crashing down. The Albert Law closed the whorehouses, sort of, while the federal indictment of the Mabray "Big Store" gang in 1909 brought an end to wide open gambling, Council Bluffs con-games, and the career of fixer Ben Marks. Marks managed to avoid imprisonment, believe it or not, and died at his home on Vine Street shortly before Prohibition became the law of the land. It's a worthwhile walk up to the grave of Ben and his wife Mary in Fairview cemetery where a bench is provided with an interesting view and place for quiet contemplation.

Made in the USA
Coppell, TX
18 December 2023